Conversation Among Stones

Conversation Among Stones

Willie Lin

❍—● ❋ ●—❍

AMERICAN POETS CONTINUUM SERIES, NO. 51

BOA EDITIONS, LTD. ❋ ROCHESTER, NY ❋ 2023

First Edition
23 24 25 26 7 6 5 4 3 2 1

For information about permission to reuse any material from this book, please contact The Permissions Company at www.permissionscompany.com or e-mail permdude@gmail.com.

Publications by BOA Editions, Ltd.—a not-for-profit corporation under section 501 (c) (3) of the United States Internal Revenue Code—are made possible with funds from a variety of sources, including public funds from the Literature Program of the National Endowment for the Arts; the New York State Council on the Arts, a state agency; and the County of Monroe, NY. Private funding sources include the Max and Marian Farash Charitable Foundation; the Mary S. Mulligan Charitable Trust; the Rochester Area Community Foundation; the Ames-Amzalak Memorial Trust in memory of Henry Ames, Semon Amzalak, and Dan Amzalak; the LGBT Fund of Greater Rochester; and contributions from many individuals nationwide. See Colophon on page 82 for special individual acknowledgments.

Cover Art and Design: Sandy Knight
Interior Design and Composition: Isabella Madeira
BOA Logo: Mirko

BOA Editions books are available electronically through BookShare, an online distributor offering Large-Print, Braille, Multimedia Audio Book, and Dyslexic formats, as well as through e-readers that feature text to speech capabilities.

Cataloging-in-Publication Data is available from the Library of Congress.

BOA Editions, Ltd.
250 North Goodman Street, Suite 306
Rochester, NY 14607
www.boaeditions.org
A. Poulin, Jr., Founder (1938-1996)

NYSCA

Contents

Thou art deceiv'd:
To hear of greater grief would lessen mine

—John Webster, *The Duchess of Malfi*

To You and For You

In the dream I was abducted, I thought sleep
would save me. That's how dumb I was, how mulish.
I thought my sleep would stop them. When the man
whispered in my ear, *If you so much as make one sound—*
the words were so soft I tried to pretend I hadn't heard
him, and his warm hand across my face hadn't disturbed me
from sleep. I thought of bees locked in amber, the curlicues
of their antennae inert but preserved in attention. I thought
hives must be fear in miniature, a swarming of infinitesimal
hooks and combs with its own scent and rhythm. Who was I
I knew I was useless, incapable in that moment of acting even
to save myself, nor even wanting to. I wanted to sleep
until the danger passed, as if it were separate from me.

Interpretive Trail

I asked for a sign.
I traveled and waited.
The heat humiliated me.
I asked for a sign that I should
before I woke. And light
arrived from a great distance,
from a great remove.
How is it that you know
what you know, I asked.
I saw the day waste away
in the corner of my eye
while clinging to a hymn, a hem
of bread. Dust gathered,
sweat matted my hair.
Like sugar dribbling down
the chin and gathering on the collar
was a sign, maybe, of
gluttony. Birds and branches
swept all one way, guided
by nature, by virtue?
Vulgar sound. Vulgar emotion.
Was this how you ordered?
Give me struggle, bruise
me with orthodoxy, if that
was your sign, I needed
to know. I ate livers and hearts.
I woke up with questions,
with eyes of bitumen.

Birth

Already, the crops are failing.
The crows shuttling back and forth,
breaking branches, dropping stones.
How easy to read sadness
into the empty room. It is yours.
All season the family has been filling
pots and jars with river water
heavy with red silt. They are tired
of that color. Cover the moon.
It is good to be inconsolable.
It is good to leave the fish uneaten,
to sing a little, sweep the floor.
Traces of breath, abundant as winter,
the uncreated memory of you.

The Vocation

And when I woke again,
I was the ant, beholden
to meat and honey, to the city,
its institution of pine needles,
straw brooms, and chalk.
I was the dog named
Black Habit. I could lift
my body in its hunger. I was
so thin I could have been
my mother in her cotton uniform
riding the bus in the rare air
of December. Pregnant
though one wouldn't have been
certain of it looking at her,
even near the end. The city
pushed its agenda of smoke.
The river ran along its concrete banks.
The stations, the secrets,
and the sun still bending
through her two brothers, through
their tangled hair, belonged
to anyone. Still. He wrote
and he wrote, too. And in the stories,
the men broke into song
as they swept snow in the streets,
each with the sudden train
of a wedding dress, or the men
slammed the table when they laughed
at their circumstance, or drank
too much to learn what it meant
to have a brother, or were true to
no end, or tried to love their fathers
before they disappeared into
hagiography. And when they pushed

the smoke out before them, it was
a nostalgic act. And the smoke
left its residue. And when they
drank, they bloomed and seemed
saturated not by blood
but by a color. For years,
and still not long enough,
they went on, flashing like wings
catching what light was
allowed, and were not inured
to burning. And there were
intervals of boredom
bred by abundance. And
there were intervals of wind,
when names scattered with
the anarchy of the unwanted
and the branch snapped,
irrevocable. And still
there were intervals
when their voices were carried
because it was good to hear
a familiar story in someone else's voice.
And when they were carried,
they were bitter to be carried
still only partway to heaven.

In the year I learned
to cease writing about history
in the present tense,
I was the silence of chalk dust,
of brothers. I was asleep
in the silence that came over people
when their dead entered,
came near. They rode past
their station. Like some animal,
the knowledge of that
moment, its meaning,

went to be alone with its hunger
where I would not
see it. There will be a need
for a catalog of such things.
There was a moment
that must be recalled perfectly
before it is cast to chance,
to meaninglessness,
and without inevitability.

Dear

A knife pares to learn what is flesh.
What is flesh.

Floating World

Somewhere, in my right mind,
I put on a mortal uniform.

Sometime in childhood, my mouth fills with salt,
a stand of trees, ink.

Year after year, walk after walk, my childhood floats with its sea.
Part flesh, part sinking stone.

A man kneels on the street.
Anyone can see him. Anyone can see that.

On our shore, the waves swell, causeless feelings. Our boys are trying to be themselves.
They need to be of use. They are practicing
to be their fathers.

The pale undersides of their arms sink into the sand.

By the black water, their shore is a palimpsest of beginnings.

The way the man kneels,
you'd think he knows something more. You'd think he is about to speak,
relieved to return to his body.

I do not want to be transformed.
I have no talent for transformation.

The boys sail out on a glass-bottom boat, but they barely manage to look down.
What's carrying them holds no wonder for them.

They grow tall and unquiet as trees.

Below us, just the sea and its noise. What we've always known
was there.

The Clearing

It was late in the day.
It was fall. It was the season
that made everything preceding it
seem mere rehearsal. Absurd
the brown, desiccated leaf
lowering itself now to touch you,
anointing itself death's emissary.
Winged lives stirred beyond.

Who are they
to believe in perfection?

You were born
to a season, and so
to a fate. In the brief clearing,
you were returned to the cellar—
down the narrow spiral passage, steps of twisted iron—
damp after rain, air drowsy
with loam, winter cabbage, and roots, and looking up
was like looking up from the bottom of a well
or staring into a new country.
Your face in the moment, unmarked by grief,
burned.

Teleology

I am finely attuned to failures.
I am an instrument of them. I accept my failings
vis-à-vis the design and accept confusion
as my occupation because I am a student, not a scholar.
This is the only world. And I am to it undifferentiated
as a lump of stone (for whom identity is not a riddle,
and I recognize the superiority of the stone in this aspect).
I am allotted an amount of daylight and that amount
shifts daily not according to my failures qua failure
but another logic. I am allotted darkness also, the effect
of which I can reproduce in part by shutting my eyes.

Object Lesson

How it began was February,
you took her by the hand, a swirling
orange-red clump of cotton batting
and everything common, to what passed
for a park in the graying city. You invented
a small mission, like searching for a dropped hairpin,
to occupy her while you slipped away
and hid, curious as to *what she would do*.
What she did was look up, at last, turn
in place, trying not to let the alarm
color her cold face, and call your name—
or what you were to her—as waxwings,
energized by the trouble, flitted, crest
to crest, their unchaste heads. The rest
you know. She decided she would keep it—
the anger that was not yet contempt
for you—like a balloon tied to the wrist,
casting its little shadow, little stigma.

Dream with Omen

A fishhead is a good thing,
to be sure—prized

for its luster one might
swallow, its dead eyes like curdled milk—

one might carry it
with consideration, one might

kiss it for luck, hold it next to the ear
for a tinny music, ask of it

in the new year, *Where is my mother?*
Am I dead meat? Give it a little salt,

blood and hair. Allow me
to demonstrate how to chew the skin

from its lip, without
a look, without a cry—how to

hang the curtains, wear a dress
white as wonder, and twirl

the fishy smell like a ring around the finger.
By the water, I lost my mother.

By the water, someone left
a fish by the pillow as I slept

with a low lamp to feel watched over.
I asked the head, *Where is the center?*

The fish meant I was exhausted.
The head was a joke, a poor substitute.

I would like to rest now
with my head in a warm lap.

Self-Portrait in White

A glazed cup.
Cotton robes.
Boiled and sugared
nests of cliff swallows.
Morning glories unfold,
shrink as if forgetting
themselves. Winter multiplies
in snow, which in falling implies
secrecy. In small intervals, the light
can be trusted to be enough
to work by. Someone
dips a whetstone in water
and slips the edge of
something sharp but not
sharp enough over it,
trying to make it
more itself.
A blade.

Apocrypha

Tell me a story about what I was
back then, show me a picture
of how light muscled through the balcony.
The windows then, I think, faced

south, though it could have been west.
For all the years I lived there, I remember none
of the rooms as mine, though one
must have been. For a time, I slept

in the storage room, whose view was of
the interior. One window looking into the kitchen.
You, too, slept in that room, before or after me.
I'll always regret it, you'd say years later,

when we are again almost strangers. In anger,
I'd ripped the pages of your notebook and
you'd struck me. I'd long forgotten. Though
when you say it, it has for me the clarion call

of truth. Suddenly I think I can recall
the blue ink, the dull light trickling in, the chair
I fell against. Back then I was always waiting for a sign.
Music always sounded somber to me,

like something heavy was pouring down
over it, keeping it low, like something was arriving
or ending, and you could say yes, something was.
I'd wanted to pull the earth—that tract

of mirthless trees, piano keys painted on
the kitchen table, the past perfecting its uselessness
like the locked wardrobe with a hole in its door—
over me like a shroud. Hard to believe now

anything so forceful, so personal
could have passed between us. Back then
I must have wanted to hurt you more than
I wanted to be whole.

Dead Dog

Step in any direction. In the cold, we become less
recognizable, though the dog
is more favored than most. He has been governed
all his years by something else. A softness.
Solitary pleasure.
Now it's his transience you touch, like touching fire without burning.
Or laughing in an unlit parking lot with the girls who were already elsewhere,
when the summer nights seemed almost mystical
in their depth and endless.
Girls who watched themselves smoke and were in love
with their hunger, nursing its secret that, in that moment, was still only
a little dangerous. A little flame,
a taut irreducibility that felt
like clarity—their whole being sharpened
into a desire. So they can say, *No, I am not thinking of human things.*

Apologia (Book IX)

Then what was she?
A door held open

＊

I always find other people's dreams interesting
Tell me about the one

＊

When she searched for it,
she found it where they said
she would:

among the dark stalks of sugarcane,
a shape
twisting to right itself

When held against the body,
it left a mark

It left her with a notion—
to be a stem of water,
to struggle under a goodly weight

＊

To describe the day by its broadest terms:

✷

The column in her pitched, taking with it
the porch, the faces—
words, too, slipped easily
through the same door
held open—gone
volume of book, gone *company*, though
the measurement for blossom
remained, a word with no English equivalent

✷

It went on, lifting and falling...

Always what was lifted felt
its fate was to be
so lifted, and what was fallen,

yes, carried
that knowledge, too

Not quite empty, the space
between them, but not containing
so when one sought logic,
there was the sense
what shadow was briefly visible had just merged again
with darkness

✷

When she started living she stopped imagining
the rowboat on water,
misplaced, and her arms heavy, though truly
she was never worried
about what happens after,
content to drift, despite the waves
—ruffled?—rustling like dread

❀

Heavily, the hand of heaven was laid upon me

❀

To carry or relinquish without
seeming to—

that was the shape it took

Admit nothing,
touch nothing—

that was the shape it took

Who did them no hurt, but gave them to eat of the lotus,
which was so delicious that those who ate of it left off caring about home

Was it virtuous—and why—to long to return,
and terrible to eat of the flower of forgetting?

The question was the shape it took,
which she turned, disbelieving, until it left its mark

❈

Wind stalked the shadows, making a lunacy of her dreams,
in whose noise of argument they had fallen

❈

I'd have chosen
to kneel, throwing my hair before me,
and to press my forehead to the ground—relinquish
with no argument

where days alight
not with rosy-fingered dawn but
fires turning, heedless

❈

Mostly, there was no choice

Who should take up the oar?
Who could believe the shadows conferring in the wind?

I, who had nothing
to say, met silence with silence

Here Is Your Portion of Eternity

An ability to gnaw
at the bone, chew the cartilage,
a patience to pare, scrape

the apple to its core,
an indifference
to blight, distaste—these were the talents

bestowed on me
by rations, by poverty.
After the body was burned, they'd find

sifting through the ashes
pearled bits of what looked like
colored glass or river stones.

Numinous, inhuman,
they thought. These must be the soul
manifest, what's left

of prayer, of purity.
They kept these in gold—
the body's detritus:

kidney stones, gallstones,
fragments of crystalized bone.
Without contempt

nor even wonder in her voice,
this is what my mother told me
of the men

sweeping the grounds.
How else go on, worrying,
worrying such a thing.

Memory

Too large—
to move it we had to
deform it.

After a while we knew
the way forward was to say
we were improved for having
moved through it, after
a while, squaring our shoulders,
lifting our hips, our heads,
then after a while longer, just
an ear, a foot.

Brief History of Exile

Now when the wind comes, I lean into it.
I'm learning to be that pure, relinquish or carry without

seeming to.
                    The things in my life
I remember with perfect clarity:

testing a pearl against the grit of my teeth,
bitter, rasped,
as I was taught; the flushed laughter

echoing between brothers
like a broken chord split between two hands;

hail darkening the corrugated blue of
a bicycle shed; the corona of the little lamp

in whose tired light sat a woman who didn't want me,
as I was taught,

                    her back dim, repeated,
framed by shelves filled with books I'd forget
how to read.

This was long ago

in another country. And always there was the sea, approaching
before receding, and the stillness
that preceded entering. Years passed

before I understood it wasn't a portrait to be finished,
perfected. It was a weight to be carried
when living, as I once did, in a town between two graves.

✺

The town where I grew up does not exist.

The man who marched and starved to get there
does not exist, though he once believed
labor is grace and the room of his anger held a stillness
like a specimen kept under glass. Now
the book of his life has turned clear:

explosive little vowels, a spray of honeysuckle,
the afterimage of the night sky burning
from his room by the bridge, the tanks and young men
riding into the city square at last...

        How much of a face is the memory
of that face? How much of hunger is
the memory of eating dirt, bark, his one leather belt?

Until his town is full of nothing,
a place where people avoid speaking
of what's passed.

They press together, sea and mountain of dark crowns.
The sky there needs no translation.

✺

In the half-light of childhood
remembered in photographs, I lived in towns

not far from here, walked the bored streets
and tried to add nothing,

wanting to be different
from nothing: asphalt, stone, the sweetness

of names like Amy and Julia that bloomed
and then grew heavy,

       —and it is easy, from here,

to see the aspect was always degradation.

Restless town, mute town,
town where traffic winds like a persistent memory
and parking lots span the years like black lungs.

The town where I was *borned*
was a lonely town, where Julia, blonde Julia, sneered,
Who wrote borned?

       Of myself
I'd thought I could live anywhere

because I've always hated your town:
that certainty was a thin, single-plank bench, where I sat waiting
in the dim light at the end of world

where I could see the gleam of another
town where I had not been at all: muted streets
through successive winters, sky yellowing
as desert sand gusted through and women
wrapping scarves around their mouths, and your
smallish fear on the back of the bicycle
as she turned, saying in a lowered voice
the warning, *mei you hao guo zi che*, diaphanous red across
her mouth, a phrase so plainly hers in those years

it's time travel just to remember it.
You don't know if you meant to remember
but it's stayed with you like a worn refrain.
Something was wrong. Something lay dormant,
slept when you slept and sprang when you woke.

＊

Walk in the direction of the stillness.

What's in these fields?

He sat lower, feeling
some of his smallness returned to him.

The river was faded
and the smog a gracelessness burning the throat.

I can't see my city,
he might have thought. To visit again
what's now placeless—

afternoons on the balcony,
that trained bird he got for his father repeating its one trick,
calling out a political slogan. Almost a joke,

zealotry from the mouth of innocence.
Parroting, like the children in school,

memorizing the humiliations they'd all learn
within this lifetime. And it's true—

the truth did not belong to them.
The denouncements and recriminations rose the same

along the weeping willows like the cicadas' nymphs
they ate in the lean years,

        wingless, unctuous,
swallowed before they could let out
what they knew.

        To have arrived is not enough.
The gray sky shifted among its moods. Suppose he thought,

I can't see my city,
the town of running dogs, where people
empty, break

not bend—where his father, his brother, a whole town
still waited to be thought of
with some tenderness.

✳

        Over a wooden table, two brothers divided
what they had left of their father. The older one
drank on and on until he stopped—became

cut silk, bits of pearl—and the other one took over, drank as if
a cry of pitilessness were at the end of the glass,
gathering and gaining
until it fell.

The sky did not fall, and between them now
they will still have the sea,

        and the music that precedes entering,
and the water wide, unable to concede
any argument.

✳

All day I felt the reproach
of the years, of forgotten words
dissolving, sugar on the tongue.

In the terrible raiment of childhood,
I tried to sit lower than myself

and looked to the sky, which returned no one.
Neither did its counterpoint, the sea.

Light lifts and it is
as if the world starts anew.

✳

Near burning,
the night is a constellation of flies.

          What forces blew through
had to learn again what rapture meant, to stand beside
one's past rising as smoke:

the kneeled one, the ill at heart, the one
who's been marching so long he forgets his own fate.
They are each being taught
how to be alone.

          In black and white portraits of the dead
they see laughter finally emptied of everything.

It's fine to keep thinking this way.

Hardheaded and soft-headed
are both ways of being stupid.

Beneath the afterimage
of towns, the birch trees were bored,
their leaves like hands pressed together
admitted nothing,

       taken over part by part
by waves of the cicadas' shuddering song, jaundiced
streetlights illuminated what was scarcely there, the ugliness of the scene
held

my head like a calyx, and the corolla, whose corollary
is language, ignited—

and memory, which is no color,
hung in the air like ash.

Living Alone

Not leaving a dropped glass unswept,
not turning off all the lights

to sleep in the dusky hum of television,
not throwing a weight against a wall

to see it break, was what it meant—I used to think,
to care for another.

Not selling all the furniture, then
losing courage, to sit among the emptiness.

Not shrugging in the cold,
nor missing the brightest hours eclipsed

in shadow, in a high room I rented
in a city I briefly knew, room whose large windows

pressed almost against the edifice
of the next building, blind to sun

except for the stray afternoon hour when the light
bent through. Not the self

that loved rules, was strict
with fate, walking into the future I did not earn,

had no right to, asking,
Was this justice? Not the one who looked

in the mirror at the bloodied lip, pausing
there, hardly there.

Not to be framed this way.
I did not believe the book

when it told me life would bring me
sorrows enough. What was it to hold another life

under one's sway? There was a time
I'd have raised my voice in argument.

In the din of youth or illness, dry, northeasterly,
swallows whipped through the willow trees

perpetually falling, scissor tails unseaming the sky,
strangers ordered themselves,

sat two and two on the train, one turning to look
in the face of a dog: a sentimental face,

not intelligent but expectant. The ceaseless
churn that only appeared effortless.

Not like that. There were old church pews, beautiful
because worn, too precious

for me, I would have for my dining table
I dreamt, before I knew.

Last Things in the Last Light

In the last winter months, the lines drawn,
the fragments of pity or rebuke, shriveled until
they were no more than the bitter salt tossed out
awaiting the latest storm. You spent so long searching
for the right word, you let go the mortal idea
as sleet fell like a chorus, steadfastness
into hardness. Once you stood in the street and watched
a house roil in smoke, for it was not your fate
to interfere. After a cold while, you thought
it'd be done with you, having held you
in awe and afraid. But for days after
you shook ash from your hair, each speck
seemingly uniform, weightless,
reduced, and from what—

About the Poem

About the poem
we'll never be certain again, forgetting already
what the friend had said, exactly,
or why—something about the soul as wick, or wisp.

How given stone, we should love
stone, given fire,
we should learn to love fire. Given the cold
alternative.

Heavy-footed from wine, I might have
sat down on the steps, leaned
into the thought.

There wasn't much to dream of.

Who could doubt our happiness?
Winter was in retreat.
All the sparrows, their noises, had gathered in the recesses of the white pine
like it was the last real thing on that street...

I remember myself
as smoke, lingering on fingertips, collars
upturned in the cold, little one.

Night a bruise I'd press to remind myself.

Apologia (Failure)

I died in my sleep last night.
Against this, I ask you to imagine a birch branch.

Shining white, a perch
for the moon stretched to a mask.

Or in place of the lie, imagine instead
persimmon trees, walnut trees, a black socket in the ground

opening into a wasp nest. Its madness
seeps into dreams like my acrid breath.

All the news is
of illness. I do not remember the name I took.

I mistook a branch's shadow on my arm for a bruise.
Like a held breath, the secret music of teeth climbs to where

there is no rest.

The stutter, stutter of hearse wheels against
the uneven winter road wakes the wasp in my pocket.

Its wings shutter like eyes
on my doll mask. They look at me, then past me.

They see what? An essential driftlessness,
recklessness. They shudder.

Pity the bruised persimmon, the green walnuts stitched
to my pockets, my nail-marks in the pith.

Too much reverence
is granted to the dead. I died

so I can say this. Tides mend the morning
and the rest of the day.

Why did the moon go mad? It heard the word once
and took it as its name.

Near Misses

—for Joe

Yesterday, again, ahead
suddenly a car drifted through lanes of traffic—
splitting the trunk of a sapling
and felling a road sign before
rolling to a stop. And you,
sure in emergencies, stopped and got out
as you had years before.
That day, like this one, exceedingly clear,
right, like so many in fall.

The way we speak of it—
as if death is the thing that happens,
and the rest, life and its attendant misses,
were nothing. I don't know my own mind?
Each time I hold a knife
I feel dangerous. All my years
so used to being spectator,
this wavering in the flash of exigency.
The world swerving
away, torn where I'd torn it.

Avenue of the Cities
—for Marni

Something shifts in the undertow.

People still smoke in the city.
Link their arms and walk two abreast

petrified, petrified. This was what I was
reading—it is the unremarkable that will last.

Cold brush of mist, silver shiver
of moon, the secret shadow

between a footstep's fall and sound.
Searching, mind of crinoline

where no wind sweeps through.
Air that is just breath repeated,

passed one to another. Far-flung
romantic notions that kept us—keep it

all—moving. That poverty was closeness,
was something shared among torched

bricks and idling cars. Touch the hand
of ghostly processions through narrowing

passages, the hand that lingered
on the balcony. Touch the hand that longed

to be held down, to strain against,
explain. The hand built of borrow.

Hand reaching backward, water
into water, that hand

and not like any hand that hit me.
(I'd hid then.) I don't know why

that should have been my idea of pain—
I was still young—something to hide

from others. A hand for that hand.

Elegy for Misremembered Things

What is ordinary sorrow?
The days settle like snow, visiting each thing, lending a sameness to their shapes.
White on white.
Heavy is the head incapable of treachery.

The days settled like snow, visiting each thing, lending a sameness to their shapes.
A missing left index finger, the man whose hand it was.
Heavy is his head incapable of treachery.
He was stern. His hair never lost its shape.

A missing left index finger, the man whose hand it was.
How many dead had he seen?
He was stern. His hair never lost its shape.
And you ask the cat, "For once, will you cease thinking of yourself?"

How many dead has the year seen?
Sand from the desert blows south until the air is full of sand.
And you ask of the cat, "For once, will you cease thinking of yourself."
It fills your mouth, it tangles your hair—

sand from the desert blows south until the air is full of sand.
You cannot sweep it from the concrete floor of the house.
It tangles your hair, it fills your mouth.
Pour water down the steps and watch it cascade, watch it dry.

You sweep it from the concrete floor of the house.
A woman strikes your hand as it moves across a cold music, ticking each mistake.
Pour water down the steps, watching it cascade, watching it dry.
You were always alone. You were never alone.

Your mother strikes your hand as it moves across a cold music, ticking each mistake.
A boy pins you to the bed and cannot explain why.
You were always alone, then never alone.
Your matching uniforms, his red cheeks.

The boy who pinned you to the bed and could not explain why.
The naked women at the public shower never stopped talking.
Your matching uniforms, his red cheeks.
The singular, fluid motion of a man in a dark blue coat as he alighted his bicycle.

The naked women at the public shower never stop talking.
You could run the perimeter of your entire world without needing to stop.
The singular, fluid motion of a man in a dark blue coat as he alights his bicycle—
his confidence in that moment makes you cry.

You ran the perimeter of your entire world without stopping.
A stranger tells you that you look like a doll. A cartoon of a girl.
Her confidence in you in that moment makes you cry.
A stranger wants to dress you in her military cap and take a photograph.

A stranger thinks you look like a doll. A cartoon of yourself.
She may never see another like you.
She dresses you in her military cap and takes a photograph.
Months later, it arrives in the mail. What didn't you understand?

She has never seen another like you.
Black and white,
months later, it arrived in the mail. You don't understand.
What is ordinary sorrow?

Memory

Afterwards there was always that weakness where the bone had been broken. Nothing could be struck again with the same force.

After an Argument

The seed danders flourish
in mysteries, in many directions
and thus are directionless.
And the beauty is enough,
for a time, to silence me,
scatter of mortal mortar,
in the widow light of dusk, almost—
or most—inured to questions,
as a matter of course, although
believing in the moment, in every
moment, there will be a price
to be extracted for such beauty—
days of cut-glass, days of fearing
whether there will be a path,
of inwardness, of confusing
proximity with desire—and in time,
the desire to be less, to be
volitionless, in the way of the world,
gears locked in perpetual toil,
turning, but not arriving,
and by turns invitation or indifference,
dandelions or snowdrift.
And in the wind, in here,
there is room, still, for smallness,
for meekness—with room, mine—
I was not surprised.
I don't know why I was not.

Little Fugues

Go out and do what you love.
It is enough.

Bring all you can carry,
what, in this life, must approximate infinity.

＊

I think I may have broken something I intended
to stay true—

     And you carrying the water
     and me carrying the flowered plates

     There was the scent of wet fabric snapping on the line
     and the questions were abstract

     Why assume that to see, finally, empty of desire,
     is to see clearly?

     When the flowers opened, it was right
     someone should stay and watch, as though the world were meant for us

The year turns its head, coolly

＊

When you read, you are full
of someone else's sadness

54

＊

Here is Greg writing *ghost*
where he'll later write *soul*.
The wind lashed—pushed,
tore down, until we felt
acted upon by what was not
force but presence. God
is direction, someone said.
Someone wept, the weeping
was full of its own sound.
We were not lost but I was lost
among them, someone said.

It was a conversation among stones.

＊

To turn the neck, stiff as light looks when it comes
through a high window

＊

Where we lived, it took a little longer
but the sun rose to take its place.

There were days when I knew brightness
as an obstacle to sleep.
I was not embarrassed to speak
of the world in such terms—
what it was *to me*.

I tried to pretend that the heaviness I bore
was not myself—

❋

In this season the wish they keep granting
is hyacinth

When I thought of my unhappiness
I was trying to make a path

❋

We thought the light passing
over us left something in us,
as it had the valley. We walked until
the light became a memory, trailing
over paths like shadows, unable
to lift our heads.

Clumsily, as in dream, we moved:
rural fog, black meadow-grass, sudden field of swans.

And that was one conviction:
that we must be to one another
what the world is not
to us. That every poem
should open to a field of swans.

❋

It is time
to see in full what you've understood only in profile,
turned slightly away, as if
toward a source of light, some idea of god:

After Masaccio's *The Expulsion from the Garden of Eden*

Scholars may quibble with the ways we take
liberties to show a rounded thing,
a curved thing, a hunched, a naked,
a rectitude, a wreckage, a memory
that tugs and strays, an enormity
settling, spilling into, entering
a narrow thing, the way air is taken in
through a mouth, the whole of sky through
the eyes, kept there. Here the boy
becomes the master of mysteries
and transforms what was wild in him
into a painting, an unsettled question.
The arch touching the air with stone,
from that heaviness, that hollowness,
fell the suffering of others. Shamed
by their nakedness, they placed their hands over
what we know is there. She has covered
her breasts and groin, he his face.
Their nakedness is as of the weight
of thought borne down, shoulders bent.
Their eyes closed to their own pain.
The angel clothed in bright robes hovers
over them sword in hand to drive them
into the new world. Wider than
the angel's wings, light still shines on them
from a source unseen, shading their bodies
in roundness, in wholeness, in beauty.
They are as transfigured—transfixed by it.
Stripped of glory, but not light,
nor beauty, nor meaning. But
it is their mouths that draw the eye:
open, unillumined, dark gashes,
shadows from which issue such hollowness,
sound as wound. Even after

all this time what surprises is how
quickly we come upon it—to it.
As darkness cannot make of itself an object,
immovable heaviness, is displaced by light.
As meaning arrives the way light does, whether
we stand to receive it. Turned away from
and turning toward it, they can face it
but not look at it, not directly. I saw it once
in a book and never forgot.

Known to All

What is sacred that is not secret?
In the wind, cottonwood leaves shatter
to sound, doe unravels roses with her teeth,
and who is to say that is not faithfulness?
Beauty indexed in body's darkness.
I drank it by the bowlful, when offered,
something to cure me, the herbs bruised and boiled,
warm and dark, darkened as if by the mystery of
their effects, sweetened enough to taste the sweetness
but not enough to hide the bitterness. What could
hide the bitterness? Disguise it.
One takes it all, arranges it.

Teleology

Day by day, the vacancies
multiplied, each one a near-perfect
circle. It was this signature that taught
her the name of what has visited her
in parts, in cameo, among the lower leaves of rhododendron,
brief and reachable, that the green leaves hole-
punched through bore the marks of the leafcutter bee,
solitary soul, unhived, making nest. And her knowing now,
some solitary business in hollow stems, in rotting
wood now admits her in the conspiracies of
its cells, now whispers in her ear. Was there pleasure
or only the poverty of the task? The exactitude
so distinct, hermetic as handwriting not one's own.
Gone when the hand is gone, not to be replicated.
Some feign that lostness, pretend
to the distance, trying for that look, as if the mind
were a spotted apple. She has seen the attitude
in photographs, smoke of bewilderment across faces, and
smiled. Brushing against sleep, breath
stirred with the humid scratching of branches, she thought,
I must thank you for bringing me
to this place, which is still not my destination.

Gauntlet for the Left Hand

I thought if I
could desire less
I could be happy.
I was moving toward
an idea. A gesture
like a field of wild
grass bending in
unison—a field
untended and there-
fore instrument of only
itself, beyond scorn,
where one bends as
others bend, not
in a single moment
exactly, but in the next
or the one before, in
agreement. When I
conjured the hand—
the flesh, casing of
skin, nail-beds, slight
tightening of knuckles
—sheathed in the glove,
gilt and fine, corrugated
as a beetle's abdomen, I
thought first not how
terrible but how true.
The steel fact kept
the man, for a time, then
kept on, after him. I thought
if *I* could possess a fact,
something true, if I could
love that truth more
than myself, I could
return to the world.

When I invented the field
falling it meant only
one place, all that is coming
to greet me, in truce,
with no ammunition.
And the moment
before that, and the one
before... I was sure
I did not care to reach
you. Name a stone
after me, I'd thought, I
would be a stone
in that field, anathema
to the field. And now,
I know it is terrible
to want nothing.

Memory

Where two met, one marked
the other, left evidence of the meeting.
Always that was the case, one upon
another, and itself touched, marked
in turn. Not ruined by it.
The hard edge of one thing against
the resolution of another.
Only the face of god remains unchanged.
Let me not fear my sorrows.

Spring in Virginia

You can choose
to have a secret or a sister. Some piano music, sawbuzz
on the verge of drowning out
what you've recovered
of yourself. The crude animals
are incapable of learning, except
by instinct. The man is a man
no worse than other men. But we want
our women more lithe,
with the simple mercy of a mouthful of bread.

There are worse ways to be a person.
I was speaking for myself.

Mercy the Horse

"Horse named Mercy freed from Florida septic tank by rescue workers,"
Associated Press (September 21, 2016)

The reeds, the tall grasses bent, holding
the impression of such weight. Such was the way
I went on, afraid to set my weight entire
on the world, shifting, distant at someone's knee.

❋

Too prone to darkness
all my life I have asked for a task,
a purpose to survive me. To be a beam
broken by a falling weight. To be impossible,

❋

like the woman in the poem, who longed to be gathered,
swept up and carried
like a pile of fallen leaves. I came to a name
as was my method: late, to everything.

❋

Mercy, if given
form, would be a storm
loosening between the shoulders, would ride, wind-borne,
to that moment beside water

❋

when, because you could not bring it closer
to you, you brought your face
closer to it, like some dog or some lower animal—
would be soft strands falling

❋

from women shorn of their hair, believing
that's where their history—loneliness—
resided, close
to the surface of things. But stay,

❋

we do not know where the forgotten reside.
In the nightmare I repeat
my mistakes—such was my mind when the eye saw
river of mercury, I read river of mercy—

❋

I climb a small gray hill
where tragedy had burrowed, made its home,
hard labor
indifferent to precision, I think

❋

joy is final,

❋

I rise, shrug off my form, I imagine
I already have what I've wanted—to arrive
at the ending, to all there was: effervescence and dread,
cries of *Mercy lives.*

Dream with Hands

This is the truth of your life, not some other,
sleep said to me when it reached me:

a lake's frozen surface
and the furious water moving below...
In that house, there was a time before,
when lifting the hours, the boxes, the faces of the ones
which I'd labeled "Memories," when I'd been surprised
by my strength. I must have looked lost, once,
shapeless as water, walking along a man-made reservoir,
surrounded by non-native trees. A wind, then and always
as if out of nowhere, showered my vision with
cherry blossoms. Flurries in my hair, my blouse,
and I felt almost a purpose, not improvising
while others performed to a script.
The way hands must feel when lifting a pail of water,
or fixed on a dipping oar, in the farness
that is not the hereafter but says, you, push harder.

Apologia (Fire)

I gave myself until the end of the bottle of wine,
I drove
        —I can hardly remember

Like anyone, I was always preparing the body
for a journey

What turn was missed—

        I barely wanted to go on

Though I tried, as if deciding between

❀

In the city where we lived, there was a place—torched,
what remained of a church—more
idea than architecture, nothing
but the walls standing

Its interior of ivy and stone more real
than any memory—

                I'd wanted to be there:
stand in it, mean laughter and drink,
watch the night sky needled with light,
the fireflies like drowning bits of stars

Whatever was left of living then forgettable
as breathing

✳

I want to give you a truth—not wing or hook—
that belongs to only you

—a thing you must contend with,
carry carefully, half afraid

to keep or set down—
a thing hard to surrender to this world,

which is barbarous country
because love and death have never been rivals here—
one always wins

I am not sorry to tell you this

You can't hide a knife in flesh
because that would be a worse crime

Hold it out, let others see themselves
in the gleam

Figures in a Landscape

We were looking for a quiet space
and found it on canvas.
You do not need guilt to rest
on a bed of nails, bed of ghostly illuminations. If asked
to describe my ideal occupation, I'd say
being marginal, speaking softly only between long intervals of silence.
A man and a woman returned
to the failure of what did not withstand a fire—
or, in another light, what the fire failed
to scour. They leaned into each other,
held up their hands, not knowing
whether to shield their eyes or dumb mouths.

I'd place us there now,
in the shape and remnant of burning.

Teleology

You want to know everything lately.
The dreamy lumber of the neighbor early mornings
in the backyard, under his burden,
sometimes dirt, sometimes tarp, fencing.
His design toward something, you know.
Snow falls like a secret between you.
The swollen door. The red ring
of sirens. The cardinals' return to the cherry tree,
not mindless but without sentimentality.
What happens despite the snow,
like Nebraska. The difficult path.
The dead squirrel. You've seen dead rats,
cats, deer, people, dutifully dressed and painted
to show pain no longer touches them,
and it's never not terrifying. Snow falls
like lost missives. Wet rings, fading.
Swinging doors, many Nebraskas,
promising infinite solitude. You will not see them
but know no bridges will lift this spring
for the sailboats' passage to the lake.
Another ritual delayed. The waiting keeps arriving
like driving snow. The ringing cold.
The world that is not ideas but objects.
Felled branch, closed door. And Nebraska is a little funeral
for you. In a dream, the knowledge flashes
neon in landscape as in a Jung Lee photograph.
You fold your arms across your chest
to keep yourself warm for a moment longer.
The weight is all you have.

Box of Stars
—*for Sara*

I hate when the gods leave us.
Field of wind, field of wine: a headache
is a loneliness in which to lie down.
So one enters sleep every night, a little softer,
learns to walk softly over graves. The brightness
in the sky neither the color of rust nor moth.
Lucid because we do not yet understand.
Though we imagine its meaning. Like a poem,
given freely and forever, made for burning.
Another season flown through. I have the one word,
the one branch I will continue to break to prove
it is mine. And I can make something of suffering
the way I can make something of elbows.

Notes

The title "To You and For You" is taken from Susan Stewart's poem of the same title.

The italicized lines in "Apologia (Book IX)" are quotations or paraphrases from Book IX of *The Odyssey*, translated by Samuel Butler.

"Last Things in the Last Light" takes its title from a line of Charles Wright's poem "Vesper Journal."

In "Avenue of the Cities," the line "it is the unremarkable that will last" comes from Larry Levis' poem "To a Wren on Calvary."

"Memory (Where two met, one marked)" was written partly in response to and borrows from Job 9.28 (King James Version): "I am afraid of all my sorrows, I know that thou wilt not hold me innocent."

"Mercy the Horse" alludes to Kawano Yūko's tanka "for instance, sweetheart," translated by Amelia Fielden:

> for instance, sweetheart—
> won't you sweep me off
> as if
> you are scooping up
> an armful of fallen leaves

"Figures in a Landscape" was written in response to Yves Klein's fire paintings.

"Box of Stars" borrows from Gregory Orr's *Concerning the Book That Is the Body of the Beloved*:

> How lucky we are
> That you can't sell
> A poem, that it has
> No value. Might
> As well
> Give it away.

Acknowledgments

Grateful acknowledgment is made to the editors of the following publications in which these poems first appeared, some in slightly different versions:

Alaska Quarterly Review: "Interpretive Trail";
America Magazine: "Mercy the Horse";
Broadsided: "To You and For You";
The Cincinnati Review: "Gauntlet for the Left Hand";
The Cortland Review: "Birth";
Dogwood: A Journal of Poetry and Prose: "Teleology (Day by day),"
      "Teleology (You want to know)";
GASHER: "Apocrypha";
Prairie Schooner: "Box of Stars";
Quarterly West: "Brief History of Exile";
RHINO: "Dream with Omen";
Shenandoah: "Object Lesson";
Southern Humanities Review: "Dead Dog";
The Threepenny Review: "The Vocation";
Washington Square Review: "Teleology (I am finely attuned)";
Zone 3: "Apologia (Failure)."

"To You and For You" also appeared in the anthology *Broadsided Press: Fifteen Years of Poetry / Artistic Collaboration*, edited by Elizabeth Bradfield, Alexandra Teague, and Miller Oberman (Provincetown Arts Press, 2022).

"Living Alone" was featured in *(home)Body*, an installation created by Cid Pearlman in collaboration with Mara Milam and Denise Leto and which premiered at the Santa Cruz Museum of Art and History.

Some of the poems in this book also appeared in the chapbook *Lesser Birds of Paradise*, edited by Éireann Lorsung and Andrea Beltran of MIEL, and the chapbook *Instructions for Folding*, selected for the Drinking Gourd Chapbook Poetry Prize by series editors Chris Abani, John Alba Cutler, Reginald Gibbons, Susannah Young-ah Gottlieb, and Ed Roberson.

Many thanks to my many classmates and teachers from these past decades, especially those at the University of Virginia and the MFA Program at Washington University in St. Louis, who continue to teach me not only through their writing but their examples.

Thank you to Lisa Russ Spaar for the APPW prompts that led to drafts of some of these poems and, of course, for the introduction to a world I could love and for showing me what's possible in poetry.

To Aracelis Girmay—thank you for the generosity and care that you brought to my work and thank you for your extraordinary work and example. To Peter Conners, Sandy Knight, and everyone at BOA Editions—thank you for your kindness and patience and for making this book a reality.

To Joe Collins—for joy, for encouragement, for sharing a life together and all it entails. *We felt we should be grateful, and we were.*

About the Author

Willie Lin was born in Beijing, China and lives and works in Chicago, IL. Her poems have appeared in *Bennington Review, Prairie Schooner,* and *The Threepenny Review,* among other journals. She's the author of the chapbooks *Lesser Birds of Paradise* (MIEL) and *Instructions for Folding* (Northwestern University Press), winner of the Drinking Gourd Chapbook Poetry Prize, and has received fellowship and scholarship support from Kundiman and the Summer Workshop Program at the Fine Arts Work Center.

BOA EDITIONS, LTD.
A. POULIN, JR. NEW POETS OF AMERICA SERIES

No. 1   *Cedarhome*
         Poems by Barton Sutter
         Foreword by W. D. Snodgrass

No. 2   *Beast Is a Wolf with Brown Fire*
         Poems by Barry Wallenstein
         Foreword by M. L. Rosenthal

No. 3   *Along the Dark Shore*
         Poems by Edward Byrne
         Foreword by John Ashbery

No. 4   *Anchor Dragging*
         Poems by Anthony Piccione
         Foreword by Archibald MacLeish

No. 5   *Eggs in the Lake*
         Poems by Daniela Gioseffi
         Foreword by John Logan

No. 6   *Moving the House*
         Poems by Ingrid Wendt
         Foreword by William Stafford

No. 7   *Whomp and Moonshiver*
         Poems by Thomas Whitbread
         Foreword by Richard Wilbur

No. 8   *Where We Live*
         Poems by Peter Makuck
         Foreword by Louis Simpson

No. 9   *Rose*
         Poems by Li-Young Lee
         Foreword by Gerald Stern

No. 10   *Genesis*
         Poems by Emanuel di Pasquale
         Foreword by X. J. Kennedy

No. 11   *Borders*
         Poems by Mary Crow
         Foreword by David Ignatow

No. 12   *Awake*
         Poems by Dorianne Laux
         Foreword by Philip Levine

No. 13   *Hurricane Walk*
         Poems by Diann Blakely Shoaf
         Foreword by William Matthews

No. 14   *The Philosopher's Club*
         Poems by Kim Addonizio
         Foreword by Gerald Stern

No. 15   *Bell 8*
         Poems by Rick Lyon
         Foreword by C. K. Williams

No. 16   *Bruise Theory*
         Poems by Natalie Kenvin
         Foreword by Carolyn Forché

No. 17   *Shattering Air*
         Poems by David Biespiel
         Foreword by Stanley Plumly

No. 18   *The Hour Between Dog and Wolf*
         Poems by Laure-Anne Bosselaar
         Foreword by Charles Simic

No. 19   *News of Home*
         Poems by Debra Kang Dean
         Foreword by Colette Inez

No. 20   *Meteorology*
         Poems by Alpay Ulku
         Foreword by Yusef Komunyakaa

No. 21   *The Daughters of Discordia*
         Poems by Suzanne Owens
         Foreword by Denise Duhamel

No. 22   *Rare Earths*
         Poems by Deena Linett
         Foreword by Molly Peacock

No. 23   *An Unkindness of Ravens*
         Poems by Meg Kearney
         Foreword by Donald Hall

No. 24   *Hunting Down the Monk*
         Poems by Adrie Kusserow
         Foreword by Karen Swenson

No. 25   *Big Back Yard*
         Poems by Michael Teig
         Foreword by Stephen Dobyns

No. 26   *Elegy with a Glass of Whiskey*
         Poems by Crystal Bacon
         Foreword by Stephen Dunn

No. 27   *The Eclipses*
         Poems by David Woo
         Selected by Michael S. Harper

No. 28   *Falling to Earth*
         Poems by Tom Hansen
         Foreword by Molly Peacock

Colophon

BOA Editions, Ltd., a not-for-profit publisher of poetry
and other literary works, fosters readership and appreciation
of contemporary literature. By identifying, cultivating, and publishing both
new and established poets and selecting authors of unique literary talent,
BOA brings high-quality literature to the public.

Support for this effort comes from the sale of its publications, grant funding,
and private donations.

✸

*The publication of this book is made possible, in part,
by the special support of the following individuals:*

Anonymous
Angela Bonazinga & Catherine Lewis
Christopher C. Dahl
Carol T. Godsave, *in honor of Jack Langerak*
Alison Granucci
James Long Hale
Margaret B. Heminway
Nora A. Jones
Paul LaFerriere & Dorrie Parini, *in honor of Bill Waddell*
Barbara Lovenheim
Richard Margolis & Sherry Phillips
Joe McElveney
The Mountain Family, *in support of poets & poetry*
Nocon & Associates
Boo Poulin
John H. Schultz
Robert Tortorella
William Waddell & Linda Rubel
Bruce & Jean Weigl